# The Art of Questioning

*How to Deliver Christian Lectures and Bible Teachings through Good Questions – a Sunday School Classic*

By Joshua G. Fitch

Published by Pantianos Classics

ISBN-13: 978-1-78987-052-7

First published in 1879

# Contents

Prefatory Note..................................................................................iv

**The Art of Questioning ............................................. 5**

## Prefatory Note

The following paper contains the substance of a lecture delivered to training classes established in connection with the British Sunday School Union. In editing it for this series of educational publications, I have omitted such portions as pertained exclusively to the work of mission Sunday-schools, and were unessential to the continuity and completeness of the work as a valuable manual for public-school teachers.

- C. W. Bardeen.
Syracuse, January 22, 1879

# The Art of Questioning

I have undertaken to say a few words to you on the "Art of Questioning." It is a subject of great importance to all of you who desire to become good teachers; for, in truth, the success and efficiency of our teaching depend more on the skill and judgment with which we put questions than on any other single circumstance.

It is very possible for a teacher to be fluent in speech, earnest in manner, happy in his choice of illustration, and to be a very inefficient teacher, nevertheless. We are often apt to think it enough if we *deliver* a good lesson, and to forget that, after all, its value depends upon the degree in which it is really received and appropriated by the children. Now, in order to secure that what we teach shall really enter their minds, and be duly fixed and comprehended there, it is above all things necessary that we should be able to use effectively the important instrument of instruction to which our attention is now to be drawn.

I have called questioning an *art.* It is so, inasmuch as it is a practical matter, and to be learned mainly, not by talking about it, but by *doing* it. We can become good questioners only after much patient practice; and, as is the case with every other art, proficiency in this one can be attained only by working at it, and*education in it only by the teaching of experience.

But if this were all I should not have ventured to make questioning the subject of an address to you; for the only advice appropriate in such a case would be, "Go to your classes, work in them, and learn the art of questioning *by questioning*."

The truth is, however, that there is a science of teaching as well as an art; every rule of practice which is worth anything is based on some principle; and as it is the business of every good artist to investigate the reasons for the methods he adopts, and to know something of those general laws which it is his business to put to a practical application, so it will, perhaps, be worth our while to dwell for a little on the general principles which should be kept in view in questioning, and to ascertain not only *how* a wise teacher should put questions, but *why* one way is better or worse than another.

Questions as employed by teachers may be divided into three classes, according to the purposes which they may be intended to serve. There is, first, the *preliminary* or *experimental* question, by which an instructor feels his way, sounds the depth of his pupil's previous knowledge, and prepares him for the reception of what it is designed to teach.

Then, secondly, there is the question employed in actual instruction, by means of which the thoughts of the learner are exercised, and he is compelled, so to speak, to take a share in giving himself the lesson. Thirdly, there is the question of *examination,* by which a teacher tests his own work, after he has given a lesson, and ascertains whether it has been soundly and thoroughly learned. If we carefully attend to this distinction we shall understand the meaning of the saying of a very eminent teacher, who used to say of the interrogative method, that by it he first questioned the knowledge *into* the minds of the children, and then questioned it *out* of them again.

Perhaps I can best illustrate the nature of what I have called preliminary or experimental questioning, by referring for a moment to the history of a very celebrated man — an Athenian philosopher — who lived more than two thousand years ago, but whose name and influence survive even in this age.

Socrates had the reputation of being a very great teacher, yet he never lectured nor preached. He had not even a code of doctrine or of opinion to promulgate. But he lived in the midst of a keen, cultivated, yet somewhat opinionated people, and he made it his business to question them as to the grounds of their opinions; and to put searching and rigid inquiries to them on points which they thought they thoroughly understood. He believed that the great impediment to true knowledge was the possession of fancied or unreal knowledge, and that the first business of a philosopher was, not to teach, but to prepare the mind of the pupil for the reception of truth, by proving to him his own ignorance. This kind of mental purification he considered a good preparation for teaching; hence he often challenged a sophist, or a flippant and self-confident learner, with a question as to the meaning of some familiar word; he would receive the answer, then repeat it, and put some other question intended to bring out the different senses in which the word might be applied. It not unfrequently appeared that the definition was either too wide, and included too much, or too narrow, and comprehended too little. The respondent would then ask leave to retract his former definition and to amend it; and when this was done the questioner would quietly proceed to cross-examine his pupil on the subject, applying the amended definition to special cases, until answers were given inconsistent with each other, and with the previous reply. Now, as Socrates never lost sight of the main point, and had a remarkable power of chaining his hearers to the question in hand, and forbidding all discursiveness, the end of the exercise often was, that the pupil, after vain efforts to extricate himself, admitted that he could give no satisfactory answer to the question which at first seemed so easy.

I will give you a translation from one of Plato's dialogues, in which this peculiar method is illustrated. There was one of the disciples of Socrates, named Meno, who had been thus probed and interrogated until he felt a somewhat uncomfortable conviction that he was not so wise as he had thought, and who complained to the philosopher of what he called the merely negative character of his instruction.

"Why, Socrates," said he, "you remind me of that broad sea-fish called the torpedo, which produces a numbness in the person who approaches and touches it. For, in truth, I seem benumbed both in mind and mouth, and know not what to reply to you, and yet I have often spoken on this subject with great fluency and success."

In reply Socrates says little, but calls to him Meno's attendant, a young slave boy, and begins to question him.

"My boy, do you know what figure this is?" (drawing a square upon the ground with a stick.)

"O yes. It is a square."

"What do you notice about these lines?" (tracing them.)

"That all four are equal."

"Could there be another space like this, only larger or less?"

"Certainly."

"Suppose this line (pointing to one of the sides) is two feet long, how many feet will there be in the whole?"

"Twice two."

"How many is that?"

"Four."

"Will it be possible to have another space twice this size?"

"Yes."

"How many square feet will it contain?"

"Eight."

"Then how long will the sides of such a space be?"

"It is plain, Socrates, that it will be twice the length!"

"You see, Meno, that I teach this boy nothing; I only question him. And he thinks he knows the right answer to my question; but does he know?

"Certainly not," replied Meno.

"Let us return to him again."

"My boy, you say that from a line of four feet long there will be produced a space of eight square feet; is it so?"

"Yes, Socrates, I think so."

"Let us try then." (He prolongs the line to double the length.)

"Is this the line you mean?"

"Certainly." (He completes the square.)

"How large is become the whole space?"

"Why it is four times as large."

"How many feet does it contain?"

"Sixteen."

"How many ought double the square to contain?"

"Eight."

After a few more questions the lad suggests that the line should be three feet long, since four feet are too much.

"If, then, it be three feet, we will add the half of the first line to it, shall we?"

"Yes." (He draws the whole square on a line of three feet.)

"Now, if the first square we drew contained twice two feet, and the second four times four feet, how many does the last contain?"

"Three times three, Socrates."

"And how many ought it to contain?"

"Only eight, or one less than nine."

"Well, now, since this is not the line on which to draw the square we wanted, tell me how long it should be?"

"Indeed, sir, I don't know."

"Now observe, Meno, what has happened to this boy; you see he did not know at first, neither does he yet know. But he then answered boldly, because he fancied he knew; now he is quite at a loss, and though he is still as ignorant as before, he does not think he knows."

Meno replies, "What you say is quite true, Socrates."

"Is he not, then, in a better state now in respect to the matter of which he was ignorant?"

"Most assuredly he is."

"In causing him to be thus at a loss, and benumbing him like a torpedo, have we done him any harm?"

"None, certainly."

"We have at least made some progress toward finding out his true position. For now, knowing nothing, he is more likely to inquire and search for himself."

Now I think those of us who are practical-school teachers can draw a practical hint or two from this anecdote. If we want to prepare the mind to receive instruction, it is worth while first to find out what is known already, and what foundation or substratum of knowledge there is on which to build; to clear away misapprehensions and obstructions from the mind on which we wish to operate;

and to excite curiosity and interest on the part of the learners as to the subject which it is intended to teach. For "curiosity," as Archbishop Whately says, "is the parent of attention; and a teacher has no more right to expect success in teaching those who have no curiosity to learn, than a husbandman has who sows a field without ploughing it."

It is chiefly by questions judiciously put to a child before you give him a lesson, that you will be able to kindle this curiosity, to make him feel the need of your instruction, and bring his intellect into a wakeful and teachable condition.

Whatever you may have to give in the way of new knowledge will then have a far better chance of being understood. For you may take it as a rule in teaching, that the mind always refuses to receive — certainly to retain — any isolated knowledge. We remember only those facts and principles which link themselves with what we knew before, or with what we hope to know, or are likely to want hereafter. Try, therefore, to establish, in every case, a logical connection between what you teach and what your pupils knew before. Make your new information a sort of development of the old, the expansion of some germ of thought or inquiry which lay hid in the child's mind before. Seek to bring to light what your pupil already possesses, and you will then always see your way more clearly to a proper adaptation of your teaching to his needs.

I said at the outset that there were two other purposes which might be served by questioning, besides this primary one which I have just described. It may serve the purpose of actual instruction in the course of giving a lesson, and it may also be the means of examining and testing the pupils after the lesson is finished. Some teachers seem to think that this last is the only use of questioning; but, in truth, it is as a means of deepening and fixing truth upon the mind that it possesses the highest value. Hence, every fact you teach, before you proceed to another, ought generally to be made the subject of interrogation.

I will suppose that most of the instruction which you are in the habit of giving in a Sunday-school is connected with Scripture reading lessons. The usual plan is to let a certain portion of the word of God be read, verse by verse, in turns by the children of the class, then to cause the books to be closed, and then to proceed to question on the lesson. Now, in my own classes in a Sunday-school, I have generally found that the mere mechanical difficulty of reading, and the fact that so much of the phraseology of the Bible is unfamiliar and antiquated, were sufficient to prevent the lesson from being understood by all the children.

So, if I reserve my questions until the end, it has often happened that many important truths of the lesson proved to have been overlooked by the children, and the result of the questioning has been most unsatisfactory. To remedy this the best plan seems to be, to put brief, pointed questions during the reading, to take care that no difficult or peculiar words pass unexplained, and constantly to arrest the attention of the class, when it flags, by inquiries addressed to individual members of it. You will also find it a good plan, especially with the younger children, after the whole lesson has been read twice or thrice by the class, to read a short passage yourself, generally two or three verses, in a slow, distinct manner, with as much expression as possible, and then question thoroughly upon the passage, exhausting its meaning before you go on to the next. When this has been done with each successive portion of the lesson the books may be closed, and the whole recapitulated by way of examination. You will find this plan answer a double purpose; it will improve the reading of the class, by giving to it a model clearness and expression, and it will enable you to question systematically on every fact you teach as soon as you have taught it. By thus making sure of your ground as you proceed, you will become entitled to expect answers to your recapitulatory or examination questions; and this is a point of great importance, for nothing discourages and depresses a teacher more, or sooner destroys the interest of the children in a lesson than the asking of questions which they cannot answer.

Thus the advantage of questioning on each portion of a lesson, rigidly and carefully, as it is learned, is, that you then have a right to demand full answers to all your testing questions when the lesson is concluded. You will, of course, go over the ground a second time much more rapidly than at first; but it is always desirable to cover the whole area of your subject in recapitulation, and to put questions at the end to every child in your class.

I have only one other observation to make as to the distinction to be kept in view between the questioning of instruction, and the questioning of examination. In the former it is often wise to use the simultaneous method, and to address your questions to the whole class. This kind of collective exercise gives vigor and life to a lesson, and the sympathy which is always generated by numbers helps to strengthen and fix the impression you wish to convey. But you must never be satisfied with simultaneous answers; they should invariably be followed up by individual questioning, or they will prove very misleading. It may seem a paradoxical assertion, but it is nevertheless true, that a group of children may appear intelligent, while the separate members of the group are careless, ignorant, or only half interested. Without intending to deceive, children soon learn to catch the key-note of a word or a sentence from their fellows, and to practise many little artifices by which knowledge and attention are simulated, and by which a very slight degree of interest may be mistaken by their teacher for sound and thoughtful work.

So, while you will often call for collective answers in order to retain the vivacity and spirit of your lesson, you should always suspect such answers; and in every case let them be succeeded by individual appeals to separate children, especially to those who appear the least attentive. Of course the recapitulatory or examination questions, should be entirely individual; in a small class the questions may well be put to each child in turn, but in a large one they should be given promiscuously; so that every learner may feel sure that he will be personally challenged, and that the knowledge of the rest will form no cloak for his own ignorance.

But, leaving for the present all distinctions as to the purposes which questions may at different times be made to serve, let us fix our attention on some points which should be kept in view, as to the language, style, and character of all questions whatever.

First, then, cultivate *great simplicity of language*. Use as few words as possible, and let them be such as are adapted to the age and capacity of the class you are teaching. Remember that questions are not meant to display your own learning or acquirements, but to bring out those of the children. It is a great point in questioning to say as little as possible; and so to say that little, as to cause the children to say as much as possible. Conduct your lesson in such a way that if a visitor or superintendent be standing by, his attention will be directed, not to you, but to your pupils; and his admiration excited, not by *your* skill and keenness, but by the amount of mental activity displayed on their part.

There is an old Latin maxim which, translated, means, "It is the business of art to conceal art." I suppose this means, that in the case of all the highest and noblest arts their results are spoiled by any needless display of mechanism, or any obtrusive manifestation of the artist's personal gifts. At any rate you may take it for granted, in relation to your art, that the best questioning is that which attracts least attention to the questioner, and makes the learners seem to be the most important parties concerned. You will do well, therefore, to practise yourselves in using great plainness of speech, and in constructing questions in the fewest possible words.

Connected with this is another hint of importance: *Do not tell much in your questions.* Never, if you can help it, communicate a fact in your question. Contrive to educe every fact from the class. It is better to pause for a moment, and to put one or two subordinate questions, with a view to bring out the truth you are seeking, than to tell anything which the children could tell you. A good teacher never conveys information in the form of a question. If he tells his class something, he is not long before he makes his class tell him the same thing again; but his question never assumes the same form, or employs the same phraseology as his previous statement; for if it does, the form of the question really suggests the answer, and the exercise fails to challenge the judgment and memory of the children as it ought to do. I may, for instance, want to bring out the fact that Jerusalem is the chief city in the Holy Land. Now suppose I do it thus: "What is the chief city in the Holy Land?" "Jerusalem." "In what country is Jerusalem the chief city?" "The Holy Land." Here each question carries with it the answer to the other, and the consequence is that they test little or nothing, and serve scarcely any useful purpose.

For this reason it is always important, in questioning on a passage of Scripture, to avoid using the words of Scripture; otherwise we may greatly deceive ourselves as to the real extent of knowledge possessed by the class. I will suppose, for example, that you are giving a lesson on the meaning of the Christian injunction, "Thou shalt love thy neighbor as thyself," and that the class has first been questioned as to the meaning of it, and proved unable to give a full and satisfactory explanation of the scope and meaning of these memorable words. The parable of the good Samaritan has been chosen as an illustrative reading lesson. It has been read twice or thrice by the class in turn, and then the teacher takes the first verse and reads it slowly to the class:

*"A certain man went down from Jerusalem to Jericho, and fell among thieves y which stripped him of his raiment, and wounded him, and departed, leaving him half dead."* - Luke x:30.

Some teachers would proceed to question thus:

Whom is this parable about? *A certain man.* Where did he go from? *Jerusalem.* Where to? *Jericho.* What sort of people did he fall among? *Thieves.* What did they do with his raiment? *Stripped him of it.* What did they do with the man himself? *Wounded him.* In what state did they leave him? *Half dead.*

Observe here that the teacher has covered the whole area of the narrative, and proposed a question on every fact; so far he has done well. But it is to be noticed that every question was proposed as nearly as possible in the words of the book, and required for its answer one (generally *but* one) of those words. Now it is very easy for a boy or girl, while the echoes of the Bible narrative just read still linger in the ear, to answer every such question by rote merely, with scarcely any effort of memory, and no effort of thought whatever. It is very possible to fill up the one remaining word of such elliptical sentences as those which have just been used as questions, without having any perception at all of the meaning of the sentence as a whole.

So, if you desire to secure a thorough understanding of the sacred narrative, it will be necessary to propose questions constructed on a different model, avoiding the use of the exact phraseology of Scripture, and requiring for answers other words than those contained in the narrative.

Let us go over the same subject again, first introducing it by one or two preliminary questions; for example:

Who used these words?

To whom were they spoken?

Why were they uttered?

Repeat the question which the lawyer asked.

What is the parable about? (Various answers.) One says, *A man who went on a journey.* What do you call a man who goes on a journey? *A traveller.* In what country was the man travelling? *Judea.* Let us trace his route on the map.

In what direction was he travelling? *Eastward.* Through what kind of country? (Here the teacher's own information should supply a fact or two about its physical features.) What should you suppose from the lesson was the state of the country at that time? *Thinly peopled; road unfrequented,* etc. How do you know this? *Because he fell among thieves.* Give another expression for "fell among." *Happened to meet with.* Another word for thieves. M Robbers. How did the robbers treat this traveler? *They stripped him of his raiment,* What does the word raiment mean? *Clothes.* Besides robbing him of his clothes, what else did they do? *Wounded him.* Explain that word. *Injured him] hurt him very much,* etc. How do you know from the text that he was much hurt? *They left him half dead. They almost killed him.*

Now observe here that the aim has been two-fold. First, not to suggest the answer by the form of the question. Hence another sort of language has been adopted, and the children have therefore been made to interpret the biblical language into that of ordinary life. Secondly, not to be satisfied with single words as answers, especially with the particular word which is contained in the narrative itself, but always to translate it into one more familiar. Children often give the word which suffices to answer their teacher's inquiry, and are yet ignorant of the whole statement of which that word forms a part. After going over verses like these in detail, I should recommend varying the form of the question, thus:

"Now, what have we learned in this verse?"

"That there was a traveller going from the chief city of Judea to another town near the Jordan, on the northeast."

"Well, and what happened to him?"

"He was robbed, and half-killed, and left very weak and helpless."

A teacher ought not, in fact, to be satisfied until he can get entire sentences for answers. These sentences will generally be paraphrases of the words used in the lesson, and the materials for making the paraphrases will have been developed in the course of the lesson by demanding, in succession, meanings and equivalents for all the principal words. Remember that the mere ability to fill up a parenthetical or elliptical sentence proves nothing, beyond the possession of a little tact and verbal memory. It is worth while to turn round sharply on some inattentive member of the class, or upon some one who has just given a mechanical answer, with the question, "What have we just said?" "Tell me what we have just learned about such a person." Observe that the answer required to such a question must necessarily be a whole sentence; it will be impossible to answer it without a real effort of thought and of judgment in the selection of the learner's words, and without an actual acquaintance with the fact that has been taught.

It is of great importance, also, that questions should be *definite* and *unmistakable,* and, for the most part, that they admit of but one answer. An unskilful teacher puts vague, wide questions, such as, "What did he do?" "What did Abraham say?" "How did Joseph feel at such a time?" "What lesson ought we to learn from this?" questions to which no doubt *he* sees the right answer, because it is already in his mind; but which perhaps, admit of several equally good answers, according to the different points of view from which different minds would look at them. He does not think of this; he fancies that what is so clear to him ought to be equally clear to others; he forgets that the minds of the children may be moving on other, rails, so to speak, even though directed to the same object. So, when an answer comes which is not the one he expected, even though it is a perfectly legitimate one, he rejects it; while, if any child is fortunate enough to give the precise answer which was in the teacher's mind he is commended and rewarded, even though he has exerted no more thought on the subject.

Vague and indefinite questions, I have always observed, produce three different results, according to the class of children to whom they are addressed. The really thoughtful and sensible boy is simply bewildered by them. He is very anxious to be right, but he is not clear as to what answer his teacher expects; so he is silent, looks puzzled, and is perhaps mistaken for a dunce. The bold and confident boy who does not think, when he hears a vague question answers at random; he is not quite sure whether he is right or wrong, but he tries the experiment, and is thus strengthened in a habit of inaccuracy, and encouraged in the mischievous practice of guessing. There is a third class of children whom I have noticed, not very keen, but sly and knowing nevertheless, who watch the teacher's peculiarities, know his methods, and soon acquire the knack of observing the structure of his sentences, so as to find out which answer he expects. They do not understand the subject so well, perhaps, as many others, but they understand the teacher better, and can more quickly pronounce the characteristic word or the particular answer he expects. Now I do not hesitate to say, that as far as real education and development of thought are concerned, each of these three classes of children is injured by the habit of vague, wide, and ambiguous questioning which is so common among teachers.

For similar reasons it is generally necessary to abstain from giving questions to which we have no reasonable right to expect an answer. Technical terms, and information children are not likely to possess, ought not to be demanded. Nor should questions be repeated to those who cannot answer. A still more objectionable practice is that of suggesting the first word or two of a sentence, or pronouncing the first syllable of a word which the children do not recollect. All these errors generate a habit of guessing among the scholars, and we should ever bear in mind that there is no one habit more fatal to accurate thinking, or more likely to encourage shallowness and self-deception, than this. It should be discountenanced in every possible way; and the most effective way is to study well the form of our questions, to consider well whether they are quite intelligible and unequivocal to those to whom they are addressed, and to limit them to those points on which we have a right to expect clear and definite answers.

There is a class of questions which hardly deserve the name, and which are, in fact, fictitious or apparent, but not true questions. I mean those which simply require the answer "Yes" or "No." Nineteen such questions out of twenty carry their own answers in them; for it is almost impossible to propose one without revealing, by the tone and inflexion of the voice, the kind of answer you expect. For example: "Is it right to honor our parents?" "Did Abraham show much faith when he offered up his son?" "Do you think the author of the Psalms was a good man?" "Were the Pharisees really lovers of truth?" Questions like these elicit no thought whatever; there are but two possible answers to each of them, and of these I am sure to show, by my manner of putting the question, which one I expect. Such questions should, therefore, as a general rule, be avoided, as they seldom serve any useful purpose, either in teaching or in examining. For every question, it must be remembered, ought to require an effort to answer it; it may be an effort of memory, or an effort of imagination, or an effort of judgment, or an effort of perception; it may be a considerable effort or it may be a light one; but it must be an effort; and a question which challenges no mental exertion whatever, and does not make the learner think, is worth nothing. Hence, however such simple affirmative and negative replies may look like work, they may coexist with utter stagnation of mind on the part of the scholars, and with complete ignorance of what we are attempting to teach.

So much for the *language* of questioning. But it is worth while to give a passing notice to the order and *arrangement* which should always characterize a series of questions. They should, in fact, always follow one another in systematic order; each should seem to grow out of the answer which preceded it, and should have a clear logical connection with it.

Much of the force and value of the interrogative method is lost in a loose, unconnected, random set of inquiries, however well they maybe worded, or however skilfully each separate question may be designed to elicit the thought and knowledge of the learners. If the entire impression left on the mind of the learner is to be an effective one, all that he has learned on a given subject ought to be coherent and connected. We cannot secure this without acquiring a habit of continuous and orderly questioning, so that each effort of thought made by the scholar shall be duly connected with the former, and preparatory to the next.

There will thus be a unity and entireness in the teaching, and what is taught will then have a reasonable chance of a permanent .place in the memory. For we must ever remember that whatever is learned confusedly is remembered confusedly, and that all effective teaching must be characterized by system and continuity. Hence, in proposing questions, it is very necessary to keep in view the importance of linking them together; of making each new answer the solution of some difficulty, which the former answer suggested, but did not explain; and of arranging all questions in the exact order in which the subject would naturally develop itself in the mind of a logical and systematic thinker.

A very good example of this peculiar merit in questioning may be found in the Protestant Episcopal Church Catechism, especially in its latter section. I do not, of course, enter here on any controversy respecting the subject-matter of this catechism; but the arrangement of the questions will certainly repay an attentive examination. Look at that portion which relates to the sacraments. It will be found that each answer serves to suggest the next question, and that the whole body of answers, in the order in which they stand, furnish a systematic code of doctrine on the subject to which the catechism refers, with every fact in precisely its right place. The excellence of the method adopted here will be best understood by contrasting it with many popular modern works in a catachetical form.

We have often been struck, I dare say, in reading the newspapers, to find what plain and sensible evidence the witnesses all appear to give at judicial trials. We recognize the name of some particular person, and we know., perhaps, that he is an uneducated man, apt to talk in an incoherent and desultory way on most subjects, utterly incapable of telling a simple story without wandering and blundering, and very nervous withal; yet if he happens to have been a witness at a trial, and we read the published report of his testimony; we are surprised to find what a connected, straightforward story it is; there is no irrelevant or needless matter introduced, and yet not one significant fact is omitted. We wonder how such a man could have stood up in a crowded court, and narrated facts with all this propriety and good taste.

The truth is, that the witness is not entitled to your praise. He never recited the narrative in the way implied by the newspaper report. But he stood opposite to a man who had studied the art of questioning, and he replied in succession to a series of interrogations which the barrister proposed to him. The reporter for the press has done no more than copy down, in the exact order in which they were given, all the replies to these questions; and if the sum of these replies reads to us like a consistent narrative, it is because the lawyer knew how to marshal his facts beforehand, had the skill to determine what was necessary, and what was not necessary, to the case in hand, and to propose his questions so as to draw out, even from a confused and bewildered mind, a coherent statement of facts.

We may take a hint, I think, from the practice of the bar in this respect; and, especially, in questioning by way of examination, we may remember that the answers of the children, if they could be taken down at the moment, ought to form a complete, orderly, and clear summary of the entire contents of the lesson.

Of course I do not mean to insist too rigidly upon an adherence to this rule. Misconceptions will reveal themselves in the course of the lesson, which will require to be corrected; hard words will occur, which need explanation; new trains of thought and inquiry will seem to start out of the lesson, and to demand occasional digression; it will, in fact, often become necessary to deviate a little to the right hand or to the left from the main path, for the sake of illustration, and for other good reasons. No good teacher allows himself to be so enslaved by a mechanical routine as to neglect these things; we must not attempt, even for the sake of logical consistency, to adhere too rigidly to a formal series of questions, nor refuse to notice any new fact or inquiry which seems to spring naturally out of the subject. Still, the main purpose of the whole lesson should be kept steadily in view; all needless digression should be carefully avoided, and any incidental difficulties which are unexpectedly disclosed in the lesson should rather be remembered and reserved for future investigation, than permitted to beguile a teacher into a neglect of those truths which the lesson is primarily designed to teach.

A good deal of the success of a teacher depends upon the *manner* in which questions are proposed. Perhaps the most important requisite under this head is *animation.* Slow, dull, heavy questioning wearies children, and destroys their interest in a lesson. It is by a rapid succession of questions, by a pleasing and spirited manner, by dextrously challenging all who seem inattentive, and, above all, by an earnest feeling of interest in the subject, and of delight in seeing the minds of his scholars at work, that the teacher will best kindle their mental activity, and give life and force to his subject.

Hence it is necessary to avoid long pauses, and all monotony of voice, or sluggishness of manner; to vary the phraseology of your questions, and to seek in every way to kindle interest and enthusiasm about the lesson. But in doing this let us remember that we cannot give more than we possess; we cannot raise the minds of others above the level of our own; and therefore it is important that our manner should show a warm interest in the subject, and that our own love for sacred truth should be so strong as to convey itself, by the mere force of sympathy, into the hearts of those whom we undertake to instruct. I have seen Sunday-school teachers whose cheeks glowed, and whose manner became suffused with earnestness as they spoke the words of healing and of life, I have seen their eyes glisten with tearful joy as one little one after another had his intellect awakened to receive the truth, and his heart touched with sacred impressions. And I have known well that these were teachers who, whatever their intellectual gifts might be, were the most likely persons to obtain an entrance into the hearts of children, to exercise a right influence over them, and to find, after many days, that the seed they had thus sown in hope and fear had been watered by the divine favor and benediction, and brought forth rich and glorious fruit. Of course we must not counterfeit an emotion which we do not feel, nor use an earnest manner as a mere trick of art, or as a machine for making our teaching effective; but a Sunday-school teacher will never be worth much unless his own heart kindles at the thought of the permanence and preciousness of the truths he has to teach, nor unless he feels a positive pleasure in witnessing every new proof of the unfolding of mind on the part of his class. Such feelings are sure to give vigor to his teaching, a vivid and picturesque character to his illustrations, earnestness to his manner, animation to his voice, and a quick, active and telling character to his method of questioning.

For these reasons I think it very undesirable for a teacher to use a book of questions, or to have teaching notes in his hand while he gives the lesson. The value of such assistance is great if you avail yourselves of it *beforehand:* if it helps to systematize your own thoughts and prepare you for the right development of the lesson. But in the presence of the children the use of the textbook has a chilling and depressing effect; it destroys their confidence in their teacher, it prevents him from feeling at his ease, and it gives a sluggish and mechanical look to the whole proceeding. Whether our questions be good or bad, it is quite certain that they should be *our own*, not read out of a book, or from notes, but growing spontaneously out of our own minds, and adapted not only to the peculiar character and requirements of the class; but also to the time and circumstances, to the special turn which the lesson has chanced to take, and to the particular inferences which the teacher feels it most important to draw from it.

For it must ever be one of the first requisites in all good teaching, that the minds of the teacher and of the taught should come into actual contact. The words of some one else, read or quoted to me, never can have half the force of the actual utterance of a living present being, whose own thought seeks entrance into my mind, and is intended specially to meet my needs. We all know the difference between reading a sermon to children, and delivering orally a far inferior address, but one attended with gestures and looks and tones which prove its genuineness. and give it directness of application. The same difference is noticeable in questioning, and therefore it is far better that a teacher should make a few blunders and inaccuracies while he is educating himself into the habit of independent questioning, than that he should be rigidly exact and careful by the help of notes or books. Swimming with corks is not, strictly speaking, swimming at all; and so the reading of certain inquiries from a catechism or a book is not, in fact, questioning at all, but an indirect and very inefficient substitute for it.

Perhaps it may be worth while to say a word or two about the answers which questions may receive. We ought not to be satisfied with obtaining a right answer from one child, nor even from the whole class collectively. In most cases it is necessary to repeat a question which has been answered, to some other child who may have appeared inattentive. And if a question is first given to one who fails to answer it, and then to another boy or girl who gives the right answer, it is generally a good plan to go back to the first child, and put the same question, again, in order to test his attention to what is going on in the class secure a hold upon the more indolent scholars only by making each one feel that he cannot possibly escape, but that his own personal knowledge of the subject is sure to be challenged at the close of the lesson. Hence, all questions should be well distributed throughout the class, and no one child should be allowed to avoid the frequent appeals of his teacher.

Wrong answers will often be given, yet these should never make us angry, but should be reserved for awhile, and shown to be incorrect by subsequent examination. Of course, if random or foolish answers are offered, it is a proof that the discipline of the class is bad, and the offence must be regarded as a breach of rule, and treated accordingly. But a mistake arising from ignorance ought never to be treated as a crime. A teacher may meet it by saying, "Will some one tell me why that answer is a wrong one?" Or, if the answer is very wide of the mark, by saying, "We will go into that presently;" or, "We will have a lesson on that subject, and you will then see why the answer was a bad one." And, in the very numerous cases in which an answer is partly wrong, and partly right, or in which an answer, though right in substance, is wrong in the mere language or form of expression, it is always desirable to alter the language of your question, to propose it again to an elder child, to add a subordinate question or two to disentangle the precise truth, and then at last the question should be repeated in its original form, and an amended answer be required. But all this implies patience and judgment; a condescension to the weakness and obscurity of infant minds; a considerate, forbearing tone; and a constant desire to sympathize in their difficulties, rather by offering a friendly help in escaping from them than by solving them at once.

It may occasionally happen to a teacher to be much vexed and puzzled because he can obtain no answers to his questions at all, or because all the answering comes from one or two prominent children. In such cases it is needless to find fault, or to complain and scold for the inattention. It is far better to look into ourselves, and see if we cannot find the reason there for our want of success. Perhaps we have allowed the lesson to proceed in disorder, and nothing is known, simply because nothing has been taught; and in this case our own method is in fault. Or, perhaps, we have been asking questions above the comprehension of the children, which they are positively unable to answer, and which we have no right to ask. Or, it may be that we have put our questions in an indistinct or unintelligible way. Let us always, in case of failure, suspect ourselves, take the ignorance of the children as a censure upon our own methods, and endeavor, with God's blessing, to turn the experience of such a lesson to good account by rectifying our plans, simplifying our language, or studying more accurately the nature of the beings with whom we have to deal.

Occasionally it will be found advantageous to vary the exercise by the employment of mutual questions; by setting the children, especially of an upper class, to question one another in turn on the subject of the lesson. They will be very shy, and unwilling to do this at first; but after a little practice they will learn to like it, and in the act of framing questions their own intelligence will be greatly strengthened. Lord Bacon said "a wise question is the half of knowledge;" and it is quite true that it takes some knowledge of a subject to enable us to put a good question upon it; such mutual interrogation as I have described will therefore be, in a double sense, a test of the knowledge and thoughtfulness of a class.

Every encouragement should always be offered to the children to put questions to their teacher, and to give free expression to whatever difficulties and doubts may be in their minds. A good teacher will never think such questions irksome or out of place, but will welcome them, and all the trouble they may bring with them, as so many proofs that the minds of his pupils are at work, and so many hopeful guarantees of future success.

For, indeed, the whole sum of what may be said about questioning is comprised in this: It ought to set the learners thinking, to promote activity and energy on their part, and to arouse the whole mental faculty into action, instead of blindly cultivating the memory at the expense the higher intellectual powers. That is the best questioning which best stimulates action on the part of the learner; which gives him a habit of thinking and inquiring for himself; which tends in a great measure to render him independent of his teacher; which makes him, in fact, rather a skilful finder than a patient receiver of truth. All our questioning should aim at this; and the success of our teaching must ever be measured, not by the amount of information we have imparted, but by the degree in which we have strengthened the judgment and enlarged the capacity of our pupils, and imparted to them that searching and inquiring spirit which is a far surer basis for all future acquisitions than any amount of mere information whatever.

www.ingramcontent.com/pod-product-compliance
Lightning Source LLC
Chambersburg PA
CBHW031440040426
42444CB00006B/903